KABBALAH

THE DIVINE PLAN

Z'ev ben Shimon Halevi

HarperSanFrancisco
An Imprint of HarperCollins*Publishers*

A LABYRINTH BOOK

KABBALAH: THE DIVINE PLAN

For information address
HarperCollins*Publishers*, 10 East 53rd Street, New York, NY 10022.

HarperCollins ®, ███ ®, and HarperSanFrancisco™ are trademarks of HarperCollinsPublishers Inc.

HarperCollins Web Site: http: //www. harpercollins. com

1
FIRST EDITION

KABBALAH was produced by Labyrinth Publishing (UK) Ltd
Design by DW Design
Typesetting by DW Design in London, England

Library of Congress Cataloging-in-Publication Data

Halevi, Z'ev ben Shimon.
    Kabbalah: the divine plan/Z'ev ben Shimon Halevi.
    p. cm. – – (The hidden wisdom library)
Includes bibliographical references.
ISBN 0–06–251304–4 (cloth)
1. Cabala - - History. I. Title. II. Series.
BM526. H35 1996   95-33027
296. 1'6 – – dc20   CIP

96 97 98 99 00 LAB 10 9 8 7 6 5 4 3 2 1

CONTENTS

INTRODUCTION

The Jewish esoteric tradition, although ancient in origin, is still alive and developing today. This is because it is concerned with the timeless problem of discovering the purpose of human life, and of showing how it relates to the universe and God. The vast body of knowledge accumulated over the centuries has undergone many changes, adapting to different places and periods, and yet the study of psychology and the path of spirituality have always remained the core of this *Hokhmah Nestorah* or "Hidden Wisdom."

Today Kabbalah is adopting the language of modern science and art to communicate its Teaching so that people can come to know what their true nature is, and thus become aware of their purpose and place in the universe. This means they can participate in the Divine Plan of Self-realization and so fulfil their destiny and be of service to the Holy One.

Opposite: Illustration from a Hebrew book of psalms. Bohemia, 1813.

Previous page: The Kabbalist on Earth interrelates with the Moon, Sun and planets and the angelic worlds beyond. At the top is a great Metatron and the Divine Name. Drawing by the author.

Frontispiece: The Way of Kabbalah. Jacob's Ladder of ascent into the three higher worlds via the nine rings of self-realization. Painting by James Russell.

TRADITION

The Hebrew word *Kabbalah* means "to receive." Some inter-
pret this as meaning a tradition, passed from one generation
to another. Others perceive it as knowledge handed down
directly from Heaven. The traditional or horizontal line of
Kabbalah may be transmitted privately, by a master to a disciple,
or publicly at a seminar. The direct or vertical mode of transmis-
sion might occur when the mystic is quite alone or even in the middle of a crowd, when an inner voice or vision imparts
the Teaching.

Kabbalah is the esoteric aspect of Judaism. The *Torah* or
Teaching is woven into the early story of the Jewish people. It is
said that the two tablets that Moses brought down from Mount
Sinai represent the outer and inner faces of the Tradition. The former was to be taught during the day, while the latter was to be
studied at night and in secret. This was to prevent any misunder-
standing by the "Children of Israel," or the immature who only
saw the exterior form of what was written, in contrast to the
"House of Israel," the elders or older souls who could discern the
inner meaning concerning the purpose of humanity and the universe, and their relationship with God.

*Previous page: Moses descending from
Mount Sinai*, woodcut after a drawing
by Gustave Doré. The two tablets of
the Law, one to be read by day and
the other by night, represent the
exoteric and the esoteric
understanding of the *Torah*.

Opposite: Prophet holding the *Torah*.
The visionary and the written scroll
are the two aspects that make
Kabbalah a living tradition.
Illumination from Maimonides'
Mishne Torah, Italy, *c.*1400.

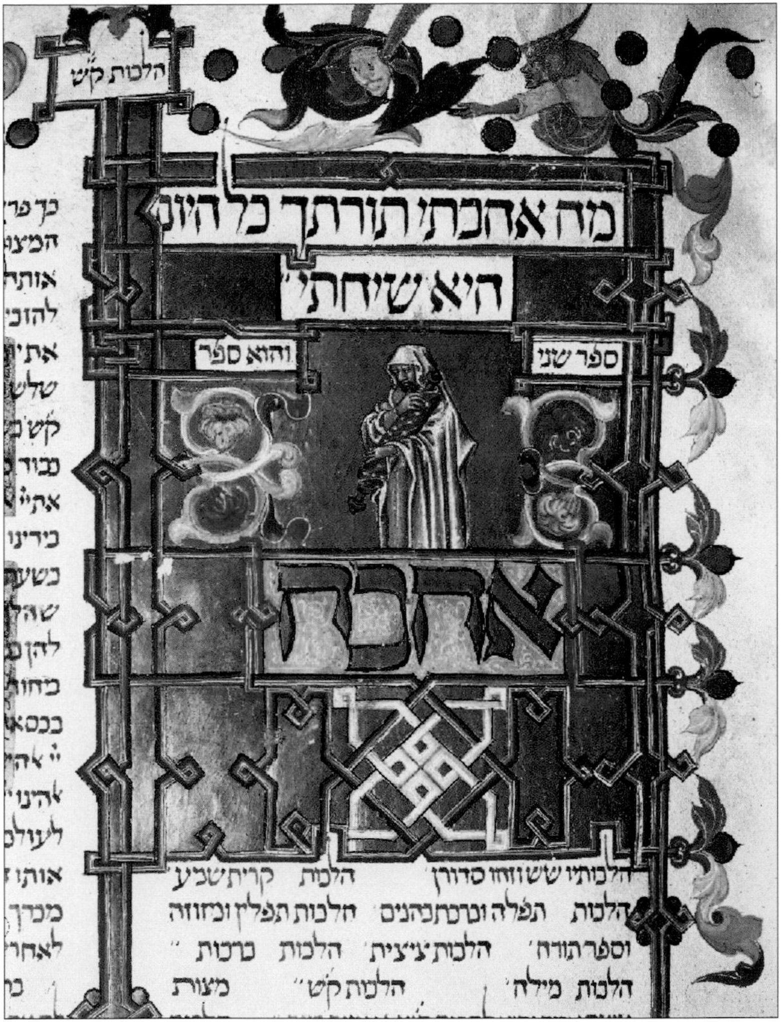
מה אהבתי תורתך כל היו
היא שיחתי
ספר שני
והוא ספר
אהבה

EVERY TIME TWO TRAVEL
TOGETHER AND TALK ABOUT
THE TORAH, THEY ARE
VISITED BY A PRESENCE FROM
THE OTHER WORLD.
Zohar

The Hebrew Bible starts with the story of Creation and its inhabitants, and with the unique position of mankind. It then outlines the earliest epochs in which humankind progresses and regresses through various stages until the advent of the patriarch Abraham. His visionary dream, which tells him to leave home and seek a distant country, marks the start of the historic period in which his descendants become a nation selected to demonstrate moral and spiritual principles. The Old Testament describes every possible human situation. Each story is an illustration of what can happen if the Divine Law is obeyed or ignored. Moses set out quite clearly the choice between the Way of Life and the Way of Death. However, there was more than a code of conduct in the Bible. Hidden in the text was much about psychology, cosmology and the nature of the Creator. To extract this knowledge required a key. That is the function of Kabbalah.

It is said that there are four ways to perceive the scriptures. The first is literally, the second allegorically, the third philosophically and the fourth mystically. In this last mode, direct cognition penetrates the simple account, the poetic image and metaphysical conclusions to bring about a personal experience of the Hidden Wisdom.

The mystical approach is the basis of Kabbalah. Over the centuries, and because of the wide dispersal of Jewry, there have been many versions of the esoteric Tradition. And yet all have, in essence, the same understanding of the myths, legends and histories associated with the Bible. The following example illustrates how Kabbalah sees the events described as part of a Divine plan.

Moses, the man chosen to lead the Children of Israel out of bondage. He symbolizes the Self which lifts the soul out of the body's domination. Illustration from the Golden Haggadah, Catalonia, *c.*1320–30.

LEGEND

The written canon deals very briefly with the fall of Adam and Eve. However, Judaism's oral tradition gives a much fuller account of the incident. Some of the spoken Teaching was included in the *Talmud*, the rabbinic record of legal discussions, folklore and miscellaneous subjects related to the Bible.

The Garden of Eden had two special trees growing within it. One was the Tree of Knowledge and the other the Tree of Life. These represent, according to Kabbalah, the higher worlds of Creation, or the realm of Spirituality (the Tree of Knowledge), and of Emanation, or the realm of Divinity (the Tree of Life). They symbolize the upper part of a ladder of four universes, in which Paradise, or the realm of Formation, and Nature, or the realm of Action, form the lower two rungs. At this point in the story Adam and Eve lived an idyllic existence in Eden, the realm of the soul. There was only one prohibition and that was not to eat the fruit of the two great Trees in the midst of the Garden.

Now prior to this paradisiacal situation Adam had been "both male and female." That is, an androgynous spirit who was made manifest on the sixth day of Creation, when the beasts of the field had appeared. The fish of the sea and the fowl of the air, symbols for the angels and archangels, had preceded Adam and therefore their leader Lucifer, the Bearer of Light, considered Himself superior to this human latecomer. Thus when the Creator asked the heavenly host to acknowledge Adam as the highest of spirits, Lucifer refused.

In order to demonstrate that a human being was the most perfect image of Divinity, a contest was set up in which Lucifer and Adam were to compete in naming animals. This proved disastrous for Lucifer, for the archangel had not been given the ability to invent or create. His humiliation before all the Hosts caused Lucifer to rage out of Heaven taking a number of rebellious beings along. They became the demonic entities who would oppose God and be the eternal enemies of Adam. When the spirit of Adam descended from the realm of Creation to become differentiated into the male and female souls symbolized by the couple in the Garden of Eden, Lucifer reappeared as the serpent. Thus this fallen creature's high intelligence was not to be wasted, as nothing is, in the Divine scheme, but applied as the Satan or "Tester" of humanity. This dark servant of God persuaded Adam and Eve to eat the forbidden fruit.

They had the choice to resist the temptation, but chose to succumb. As a result of eating of the Tree of Knowledge, they became aware of the power of free will and good and evil. In order to prevent them partaking of the Divine Tree and becoming immortal, before being responsible, they were sent down to the lowest, material, world to put on coats of skin, that is to be born and take on fleshly bodies.

The descent of humanity was part of a plan in which Adam and Eve were to become the organs of perception for the Divine. Their evolutionary ascent and exploration of Existence while returning to the Absolute was to be the instrument by which God beheld God in a journey of Self-realization. The recognition of this role can only be seen by penetrating the symbolism of the story.

Opposite: The Garden of Eden— the world where Creation takes on form and the androgynous, spiritual Adam divides into male and female soul mates, the symbol of humanity. Part of a triptych by Hieronymus Bosch, *c.*1450–1516.

HISTORY

Book was given to aid Adam on his *Teshuvah*, or return, by the archangel Raziel, whose name means "Secrets of God." This was passed on to the early generations of mankind. Unfortunately it was misused, as in the case of the "sons of God," the more spiritually advanced, who seduced "the daughters of men," the less evolved. They bore shrewd monsters who preyed upon everyone. This abuse and other arrogances almost brought about an end of the human race, whose wickedness was curtailed in the Flood. Fortunately, the line of righteousness had been maintained by Enoch who, according to legend, was taken up into Heaven during a meditation and shown the reason for Existence. He was the first fully Self-realized person and became, upon transfiguration, the great being "Metatron." As such he took on the role of Teacher of Teachers as well as filling the place in Heaven vacated by Lucifer.

Enoch, "the Initiate," reappears in the Bible as Melchizedek the priest-king who, it was said, had neither father nor mother. It was he who gave Abraham the Teaching at Salem (Jerusalem) about 1800 years before the common era. Enoch was to manifest himself later as Elijah, the secret instructor and protector of great Kabbalists. He also appeared in many other forms down the centuries to help deserving people, as he was a master of time and space.

Previous page: Enoch, the one who did not taste death but was taken up into Heaven and transfigured into the human archangel Metatron. *Ascension of Enoch,* by Nicholas of Verdun, *fl.* 1150–1200.

Above: An angel or messenger. These non-physical beings inhabit the higher worlds. Each one has a task in the Universe and belongs to a particular Order.

WHEN I ASCENDED INTO THE
HEAVENS I SAW THE HOLY SONS
OF GOD MOVING IN FLAMES OF
FIRE, WEARING WHITE CLOTHES,
WHOSE COUNTENANCES SHONE
LIKE SNOW.
Ethiopian Book of Enoch

Abraham was the first of a line that was to generate three great religions of revelation. His name means "Father of Nations or Traditions." The Torah was passed on to Isaac and his son Jacob, whose transformation into Israel indicated a shift from the psychological or personal level to the spiritual or cosmic viewpoint. One of his children, Levi, carried on the line of knowledge and it was into the tribe of Levi that Moses was born around the thirteenth century B.C.E. The descent into Egypt and slavery, which symbolized being bound by physicality, was followed by the Exodus and ascent through the desert before coming to the Land flowing with Milk and Honey, or the realm of the Spirit. Moses was shown the secrets of Heaven on Mount Sinai. These were embodied in the form and rituals of the Tabernacle and Solomon's Temple. The latter structure, built in the tenth century B.C.E. with its outer and inner court, sanctuary and Holy of Holies, for example, represented the four worlds of Action-*Asiyyah*, Formation-*Yezirah*, Creation-*Beriah* and Emanation-*Azilut*.

Melchizedek, the righteous king who had neither father nor mother, but was a manifestation of Enoch when he visited Earth to initiate Abraham. By Dirk Bouts, Netherlands, *c*.1464–7.

David, the King, and model for the Messiah, which means "the Anointed One." This title was reserved for whoever was the most spiritual person in each generation. Illustration from a Hebrew Bible and prayer book, northern France, late thirteenth century.

Alas, even the wise Solomon, called master of the three lower worlds, could be tempted. He permitted Pharaoh's daughter to place an Egyptian sanctuary in the Temple and be outwitted by the evil Asmodeus, King of the Demons. For a time he became a wandering madman, while the demon sat on his throne. These and other errors caused the eventual dismembering of his kingdom, the symbol of the ideal civilization. Despite many prophetic warnings, later kings infringed the Torah. This led to the inevitable destruction of the First Temple in 587 B.C.E. and the first dispersal of the Jewish people.

The exile in Babylon in the sixth century B.C.E. brought about a new formulation of the Hidden Wisdom, influenced by Babylonian, Persian and Greek mythology and philosophy. Ezekiel, a priestly visionary, presented Existence in terms of a huge Chariot bearing a great Throne upon which sat a vast fiery human figure. This mystical symbol became the model for what was called the *Hekalot* tradition of the "Heavenly Halls," which appeared in the centuries prior to the Common Era. In this the *Merkabah* or "Chariot" riders entered the higher realms during deep meditations. Out of these inner journeys came many accounts of the invisible regions and their celestial inhabitants. Some great mystics claimed to have seen the fiery figure of the Divine Adam and even to have encountered and talked with Metatron.

Elijah ascends in a fiery chariot. He appears over the centuries as another manifestation of Enoch. A teacher and supporter of spiritual people, he would appear and then disappear after completing his mission. Serbian icon, Belgrade.

The esoteric tradition was brought to Italy from the declining Oriental rabbinic academies in the ninth century and a little later via North Africa to Spain. From these places it spread to Germany, France and beyond. Here it underwent a major transformation, due to the conflict between religion and philosophy in the Judeo-Arab world in the thirteenth century. When the issue of Revelation versus Reason seriously began to split Jewry, the usually discrete circle of mystics of Gerona in Catalonia thought that Kabbalah might reconcile the two Truths. This group, which included the great Rabbi Nahmanides, produced a Neo-Platonic system of thought based upon the secret doctrine of Isaac the Blind of the French school, who disapproved of its publication. However, such objections were too late, especially when the encyclopedic *Book of the Zohar*, edited by Moses de Leon, became a best seller. This massive work not only revolutionized Jewish religious attitudes, but spread out widely to influence many European intellectuals such as the Renaissance scholars Pico della Mirandola, Reuchlin and Agrippa. From this, in the sixteenth and seventeenth centuries, came Christian Kabbalah, the Rosicrucians, the Freemasons and the Western Occult tradition. The four-suit Tarot pack of cards, for example, is based upon the four Kabbalistic worlds, while the Major Arcana relates to the twenty-two Hebrew letters.

Jewish calendar. To everything its season: cycles of the moon divide the year, the phases of physical and spiritual development are a continuing spiral. Illustration from a Hebrew Bible manuscript, Spain, 1301.

Jewish Kabbalah underwent another major change, in the sixteenth century, when Isaac Luria, who believed he was the Messiah, introduced his personal ideas at the Kabbalistic center of Safed in Ottoman Palestine. Although his concept of shattered vessels and displaced worlds was contrary to the Torah, in which God clearly said that all Creation was *tov meod*, "very good," his explanation of evil in the world was widely accepted. This was because of the continuous persecution of the Jews and their recent traumatic expulsion from Spain in 1492. Lurianic Kabbalah became the popular version of the Tradition, while the original line of Moses Cordovero, his teacher, carried on as the "Hidden Wisdom." In the seventeenth century, Kabbalah was used to support the claim of the false Messiah Shabbetai Zevi. When, on being given the choice of conversion or death, he became a Moslem, causing the collapse of a mass movement, the study of Kabbalah was forbidden to all but the learned and wise. It remained this way until its revival in the late twentieth century as a spiritual path for many seeking a meaning beyond materialism.

Amulet against the Evil Eye. Theurgy, or magic, crept into Kabbalah as its practical aspect, quite separate from the theological evolution of the tradition.

IMAGE OF DIVINITY

What then is the Kabbalistic system and its methods? First there is the Teaching concerning God. According to a medieval school, the Holy One is beyond Existence. Indeed it can be said that God does not exist. To clarify this seeming contradiction they used two philosophical terms: *Eyn,* which means "No-thingness," and *Eyn-sof,* which can be translated as the "Limit-less." Both are definitions of ways of looking at the Absolute. One indicates Non-existence and the other, as that which contains All-existence.

In the great Kabbalistic work the *Zohar,* it states "Face did not gaze upon Face." By this is meant that the Holy One was totally alone, for nothing else existed. However "God wished to behold God," Tradition says; therefore a mirror had to be brought into being to make a reflection. This speculum is Existence. Others say that God wished to be known. What ever the reason, it was by an Act of Will that a process was begun to bring a series of universes out of the Absolute.

A start was made, according to Kabbalists who tried to explain the unexplainable, by the Omnipresent retracting, to allow a minute space to emerge. This void was to be the vessel that would be filled by Existence. When Moses asked what Holy Name he should use, to convince the Israelites that he had the authority of God, he was initially given *Eheyeh* or "I am." Then came *Eheyeh asher eheyeh* —"I am that I am." This is not only a title but an intention, for it contains the reason for Existence. First there is "I

Previous page: Adam Kadmon was the primordial image of the Divine. This vast figure was the reflection of God. Sometimes called the Power and the Glory, Adam Kadmon was the origin of all human beings. This is expressed in Hildegard's vision of the construction of the world.

Left: Moses is given the Teaching on Mount Sinai. It is passed down to the Elders and then on to the Children of Israel to act as a guide and set of laws for righteous conduct. Illustration from the Regensburg Pentateuch, southern Germany, *c.*1300.

> COME AND SEE. WHEN THE HOLY
> ONE, BLESSED BE HE, WISHED TO
> BRING FORTH THE WORLD, HE DREW
> A SPARK OUT OF THE DARKNESS
> AND IT BEGAN TO SHINE.
> Zohar

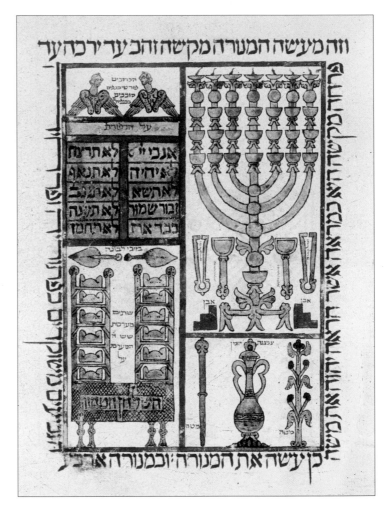

The ritual implements of the
Tabernacle. They had a function in the
priestly rituals which were ceremonially
performed in front of the Children of
Israel, except for the esoteric rites in
the sanctuary and Holy of Holies.
Illustration from the Perpignan Hebrew
Bible, France, 1299.

Opposite: The Divine Name JHVH.
When this fiery title was written in a
vertical mode, it made the image of
Adam Kadmon appear, hence its highly
restricted use. Author's calligraphy.

am," the Source of Being, then comes the word "that." This relative pronoun represents relative Reality which will mirror the second "I am" as a reflection. The composite statement defines the emergence of God's Will coming out of the Absolute to bring about a Manifestation in which Face can gaze upon Face. The Divine image is beheld in the returning reflection of Self-realization. "I am" is the Eternal Self.

The last Name given to Moses, as the one to be used by the Children of Israel, is the sacred Tetragrammaton, consisting of the consonents *YHVH*. This was later to become graphically converted into Ezekiel's Fiery Man, known as the *Kavod*, or the Glory, when the four letters were set out vertically. As such they formed a human figure, called by Kabbalists *Adam Kadmon*, the Primordial Man. This Divine image both revealed and concealed the Absolute in a coat of Pure Light.

In the *Sefer Yezirah*, a book from about the sixth century, the term the ten *Sefirot*, or numbers, is used. These are seen as the ten Divine principles that were emanated out of No-thingness to generate the paradigm upon which Existence would be based. They form the anatomy of Adam Kadmon, and represent the various levels and functions within a unity. The Sefirot were also seen as a Tree of Divine Lights. This concept probably came from the Menorah, the seven-branched candle stick in the Sanctuary of the Tabernacle and Temple, which had seven lights, three joints and

twenty-two decorations. They became the basis of the Tree of Life diagram that appeared in medieval Spain.

This first Divine level was called by Kabbalists the world of *Azilut*, which means "to be next to." The philosophical mystics saw it as the realm of Emanation and potentiality. Here was the dimension of Eternity, the prototype of the three lower worlds yet to come into being. Indeed, some Kabbalists saw it like a tree that grew upside down so that its roots were in the Absolute, while its trunk became Creation. The branches were seen as the Garden of Eden or Formation and the leaves and fruit the lowest world of Action. The totality of the worlds constituted, in their integrated mode, a vast mirror frame in which the Absolute could contemplate its reflection.

Opposite: The origin of Existence. Absolute Nothingness and Absolute All wills the ten Sefirot, or Divine Principles, to come into being. At first they fill the space vacated by the Holy One to allow Somethingness to be manifested. Drawing by James Russell.

JACOB'S LADDER

The ten Divine Attributes were given various symbolic names according to their qualities. The first and highest was *Keter*, the Crown, source of all. Then came the two side supernals, *Hokhmah*-Wisdom and *Binah*-Understanding. These corresponded to the brain of Adam Kadmon. Below these two outer pillar Sefirot were *Gevurah*-Judgment and *Hesed*-Mercy, the emotional principles of fear and love. These constituted the heart of the primordial Adam. Beneath and between these came *Tiferet*-Beauty, symbolizing the pivotal point at the center of the Divine realm. This was on the central column of Grace descending from *Keter* and midway between the top and bottom of the Sefirotic Tree. Under the solar plexus of the first Adam (*Tiferet*) came the two Sefirot of Action, *Hod* and *Nezah*. These are usually translated as Glory and Victory, but this is misleading as their root words mean "to shimmer or vibrate" and "repeat or cycle" respectively. They are sometimes seen as the hands or legs of Adam Kadmon. The last two, on the central column, are *Yesod*-Foundation and *Malkhut*-Kingdom. The former represents sex, to some Kabbalists, and the ordinary mind to others, while the bottommost Sefirah is seen as the sum total of all the rest, or the Divine vehicle or body as a whole.

Opposite: The Tree of Life. Here the medieval Kabbalist has arranged the ten Sefirot into a metaphysical configuration. The various Divine qualities have been set out in a specific order to express the paradigm of existence.

There is also what is called the non-Sefirah of *Daat*-Knowledge that occupies the central space below the three supernals. This is considered the place of the *Ruah ha-Kodesh*, the Holy Spirit, sometimes called the Voice of the Logos—the Word of God.

The world of the Divine holds past, present and future. It is the realm of timelessness, because all are contained within the totality of the Eternal Now. However, in order for God to behold God, there has to be an extension of Existence, otherwise there would be no time or space in which all the dimensions of Divinity could be experienced. There had to be movement, a going out from the potential to the actual. This was to take the mode of generating multiplicity from the primordial world of Unity, thus developing, as Existence extended, an increasing diversity that would eventually seek to return to a union with its origin in the One, the Ancient of Ancients, as the Absolute was also called.

According to tradition, each of the twenty-two decorations on the seven-branched Menorah has a Hebrew letter associated with it. They represent the connections between the ten Sefirot. Letters

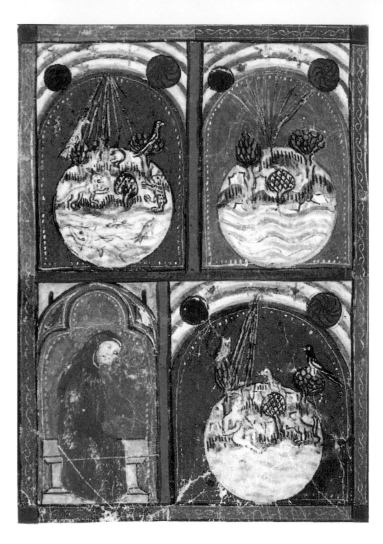

The seven days of Creation move existence out of the eternal world of the Divine and into time. This motion will not end until the creative and evolutionary process is complete. Illustration from the Sarajevo Haggadah, Catalonia, fourteenth century.

Opposite: The Fall from Grace, by Hugo van der Goes, *c.*1440–82. The conventional view is that Adam and Eve fell from grace. A Kabbalist would say that their descent was planned by the Almighty so that the human couple could begin their journey of ascent towards self-realization.

make words and words sentences and so on. In this way various combinations of the *Aleph-Bet* would bring about differentiation. When the Creator said "Let there be light," it precipitated Creation, in which the division of Day and Night set up the two outer, positive and negative, pillars of a new and lesser universe. On the Second Day came the separation of the firmament, or the extraction of the cosmos of *Creation*-Beriah from the realm of Emanation. Thus the first of the three lower worlds began to emerge. The Third Day added Water and Earth to the Air of Creation and the Fire of the Divine world. This Day also established "Life" in the manifestation of plants. On the Fourth Day the celestial lights and the cosmic rhythms were brought forth, while the Fifth Day saw the creation of the fowl of the Air and the fish of the Sea. Archangels lived in Creation, which is a gaseous world, while the angels would exist in Formation-*Yezirah*, which is a fluidic universe. On the Sixth Day came the beasts of the field, the Earth-bound solid creatures, and a second, "Spiritual," Adam. The last Day was devoted by the Creator to rest and was the first Sabbath for reflection upon *Beriah*.

Out of this world of Beriatic Ideas, as Platonists would call it, came the seven Halls of Heaven that would figure greatly in Hekalot literature. Here is where the essence of every creature was to be found. Their "forms" were to become manifest in the next world of *Yezirah* that now emerged. Here in the Garden of Eden was every shape and size of stone, plant and animal that would eventually be seen in the realm of Nature. It was in this world of Formation-*Yezirah* that the Spiritual, androgynous Adam became divided into the twin souls of Adam and Eve. Here they resided until they were tempted and had to go down into the lowest world, that of material manifestation—*Asiyyah*, where the mineral, vegetable and animal entities entered into the four states of matter. Here time was the fleeting "present" ever moving on, always changing in contrast to the Eternal "Now." And yet, although encased in spirit, psyche and body, Adam and Eve contained a spark of Divinity and the possibility of redemption.

When Jacob dreamed of a great Ladder stretching from Earth to up on High, he saw the Great Chain of Being. He also saw *Melechai*, messengers, going up and down, indicating two processes—one coming from above, the other from below. Some Kabbalists see this as the descent of souls to Earth to be born and the ascent after death. Others regard the going up as the return to the Divine. Kabbalah teaches that each

human being is a cell in the body of Adam Kadmon which comes down as an innocent into the three lower worlds to gain experience in order eventually to reunite with the Divine Adam and impart what has been learned. This process will continue until Adam Kadmon is aware of every nook and cranny of Existence. In this way the three lower worlds become a three-dimensional reflection that synthesizes into a single Self-conscious image. To help this happen is the aim of Kabbalistic practice. Some traditionalists call it *Tikkun* or "restoration," others speak of it as redemption. The object is the same—individual and collective Evolution.

Opposite: Jacob's Dream of the Heavenly Ladder, by Hans Bol (1534–93), seen as the spiritual staircase between the upper and lower worlds. On it, beings— messengers—ascend and descend. Meditation was seen as a method by which the Kabbalist could gain an insight into the above.

ANGELS AND DEMONS

According to Kabbalah, there is a profound difference between the angelic entities and human beings. The former were created during the first Seven Days, whereas humanity existed before them as the sparks of Divinity. This gave humans the unique ability to operate at every level. Angels and demons, however, were confined to specific worlds and functions because they had no free will to do as they pleased. If they had, there would be total chaos in the universe. A Kabbalistic myth illustrates why.

When the angels were asked by the Creator their opinion about the desirability of bringing Adam into Creation, those on the right and merciful side of Heaven said it would be good, while those on the left and judgmental side considered it bad. Each order only saw from its viewpoint, even as human optimists and pessimists see life according to their temperament. Lucifer, as noted, objected to Adam's introduction into Creation, while Great Michael and Gabriel, who also held central but lower positions in the archangelic hierarchy, said Adam would add to the glory of Existence.

When the rebellious angelic powers left Heaven, their desire for destruction became a vital function, as someone in the universal system had to take on the task of breaking down and destroying whatever is redundant, bad or dead. As bacteria and vultures have their place in disposing of decaying matter in Nature, so the demonics have the job of decomposing non-physical elements and

Previous page: The Archangel Michael, from a tenth-century Byzantine panel, now in St. Mark's, Venice. There were many Orders of Angelics, called Armies, Legions and Cohorts. These were led by officers, called Archangels, of various ranks

Above: The Demonics were those Angelics who rebelled with Lucifer against God when the spiritual Adam was seen to be superior to all other creatures, even though he was the last to emerge in Creation.

Left: The fallen Lucifer became Satan the "Tester," or adversary of humanity. As the Devil, it represented evil—the tempter and tormentor of Mankind. Hildegard's vision of the Powers and Principalities.

> THE MASTER REBUKED HIM
> SAYING EVERYTHING CREATED
> SERVED GOD'S PURPOSE, EVEN
> THAT WHICH SEEMED A THREAT
> TO MAN HAD ITS PART IN
> CREATION.
> Zohar

situations that are dying or diseased. This is why Satan is sometimes seen as the Angel of Death. Kabbalists avoided encountering such sinister creatures during their excursions into the invisible realms. Lucifer, however, could not be so easily sidestepped. Satan's role was to test the integrity of mystics by tempting the shadow side of their psyche or puffing up any spiritual pride. The Book of Job is all about this examination.

The lowest of the angelic entities are the Nature spirits. These watch over places such as rivers, forests and mountains and species of plants and animals. There are also the elementals who are responsible for the weather. Each deva has its occupation written upon its forehead. This always ends with the word *El*-God, to

Gabriel, the Warrior of God, was the guardian of the gate of Heaven. He was also the Annunciator, the Archangelic power who brought the Word of the Holy Spirit, the Voice of the Divine. Mural, c.1340, Decani (former Yugoslavia).

remind them who they serve. Thus the angel that manufactures snow is called Shalgiel, while the angel of lightning is called Barakiel. These beings can only act if the conditions are right for their manifestation.

The higher angelics are organized into hosts of the right, left and middle pillars. They are subdivided into cohorts and legions with ranks of command officered by archangels. Much of this information has been passed down from the time of the Babylonian Exile, but considerable knowledge was gleaned from the mystical ascents into the Hekalot Halls by the Merkabah riders of later schools, such as those of the Pharisees, the priests, and probably the Essenes. Some of these described the angelics in their visions as vast winged beings, cosmic wheels with eyes, and as luminous faces and bodiless voices. The worlds of Formation and Creation have as varied a population as any Earthly habitat.

The most well known archangels are Michael, Gabriel and Raphael. They guard the gates of Heaven and perform particular functions. Michael is the captain of the Heavenly Hosts and the high priest of the Celestial Temple, while Gabriel is the original guardian angel and annunciator of the Divine Will. Raphael represents the principle of spiritual healing. There are also what are called the four Holy Living Creatures. The one in

Metatron, or Enoch, was the first fully Self-realized individual. He took the place vacated by Lucifer's fall as a human being with Archangelic powers. Metatron, the Prince of the Presence, was the Teacher of Teachers, as well as the Regent of God. Late Byzantine panel, Constantinople.

Opposite: The four Holy Creatures supported the throne of Heaven. The Bull, Lion, Eagle and Man symbolized the four worlds of Action, Formation, Creation and Emanation. They were the celestial principles of Earth, Water, Air and Fire. Illustration from Maimonides' *Leader of the Undecided Ones*, 1348.

the form of a Man represents the Divine, while the Eagle-like being symbolizes Creation. The Leonine archangel watches over Eden, even as the great winged Bull supervises the physical realm. These four spiritual watchers hover around the Throne of Heaven, while an archangelic entity called Sandalfon acts as intermediary between all the worlds. This is because, it is said, Sandalfon is another manifestation of Metatron, but at a lower level, for the name means "co-brother" or "co-operator." Legend says that Sandalfon makes wreaths of prayers and hands them up to the Holy One. This unique position is possible because, the Tradition adds, Sandalfon is so tall that he can reach all the way up Jacob's Ladder. Such stories are full of esoteric implications. The *Zaddik* or righteous human being, for example, has the ear of God, which is why many ordinary people would ask the saint or sage to offer a petition to the Holy One on their behalf. This is because they have the ability to enter the higher worlds and touch the Divine level. Such a capacity is possible for a developed individual who is a microcosm of Existence, the "Face within the Face," as some Kabbalists say.

HUMANITY

Previous page: Here the souls of the wicked descend into Hell, but there is another stream ascending into Paradise and higher into Heaven. Between is Purgatory, the place of cleansing that occurs after death. The level attained is determined by the individual's use of choice or free will. Illustration by Gustave Doré from Dante's *Inferno* .

Opposite: The Wheel of Life and Death, by Hildegard of Bingen. In Kabbalah it is called *Gilgul Nefashot,* the cycle of reincarnation in which a soul develops over many lifetimes.

umanity is unique. It is unlike any other creature because besides possessing free will it has, as was said, the power to enter or be conscious of all four worlds. Every human being comes from a particular limb or organ of Adam Kadmon. This is a symbolic way of saying it has a specific purpose. As a cell of Divinity with a preordained purpose, each individual descends into Creation with the cry "I am" as it enters Time. Here the human entity becomes enwrapped in a spirit. It then passes down through the seven Heavens to enter the realm of Forms where it is divided and enclothed as two separate but complementary psyches, one male and one female. They are also part of a soul group which has its root in a certain limb, organ or function of Adam Kadmon.

According to the *Zohar*, the mates and their companions reside in Eden or the Treasure House of Souls, as it is called, until their time for incarnation has come. Very reluctantly they all leave Paradise and go down into the physical world to be born. Here begins a long journey back to the Source. At first they live together, but later they all disperse in order to gain experience. When they reach the level of individual maturity, they meet again and join up with the others to carry out their part of the Divine plan in which they turn their lives and work into a reflection of the Holy One.

Needless to say, one lifetime is not sufficient to complete the training and mission of each individual. According to Kabbalah, the cycle of transmigration of souls, called *Gilgulim* or Wheels, is necessary to fulfil one's destiny. Moreover, soul mates often have to be apart so as to learn important lessons before they can unite as a wise and reliable couple who can carry out their joint spiritual function. Because of free will and inevitable errors, the reunion is often delayed as karma, or *Midah ke-neged Midah*, "Measure for Measure," as Kabbalists call it, is worked out. The searching for the soul mate is part of this process and when all things are ripe the two partners meet and unite.

Between lives the disembodied individual returns to the upper worlds, first to go through a reflective purgatorial period of cleansing, and then to an appropriate level. This might be *Gehenna*, or Hell, the place where persistent sinners are isolated and endure each other's unpleasant company. Or it might be what is called the Earthly Paradise, where the Garden of Eden is the background to a well-earned rest. Some more advanced souls might ascend to the Heavenly Paradise, where a more refined order of life after death is lived. Yet others, those who have developed their spiritual capability, can rise to reach one of the seven Halls of Heaven, where what are called the Academies on High are presided over by eminent teachers.

The time spent in the upper worlds depends on many factors. In most cases it is a generation, so that members of a soul group can all reassemble and then descend to Earth at the same time and so continue their collective development or work out their karmic fate. The more advanced individuals or groups, who have learned to live in the spirit, can choose when and where to be reborn for specific missions. These are the great men and women who make history. At the other end of the scale are such people as suicides, who are trapped in a limbo between the living and the dead. They appear as ghosts or *dybbuks*, who seek to resolve their problem by haunting the places where they died or by taking over susceptible people whom they try to possess in order to reenter physicality without going through the necessary post-mortem or pre-natal processes. As can be seen, a vast process is in progress as human beings descend and ascend Jacob's Ladder. This panorama is described in the *Book of Enoch*, a work from the Hekalot period, in which Metatron showed a certain Rabbi Ishmael a huge cosmic curtain, the *Pargod*, hanging down from Heaven. Its pattern represented the overall form of history from the Beginning of Time until the End of Days when the Divine plan would be complete. The individual threads that made up its fabric showed the sequence of fates that a person would live in order to learn how to execute their destiny.

There were many qualities of thread, some gold, some silver and others of every kind of fiber. However, each one had its place in a

AT THE SEVENTH LEVEL I MET THE SOULS OF THE RIGHTEOUS AND SAW THEM ENJOYING HEAVEN'S DELIGHTS AS WE WERE SHOWERED WITH BLESSINGS OF PEACE, BENEDICTION AND GRACE.
Zohar

Opposite: The world of Heaven. This level of spiritual reality was reserved for those who had persevered in righteousness and had earned a place in the realm of peace. *The Plains of Heaven*, by John Martin, 1851–3.

49

Opposite: Adam, or all Mankind, was created in God's image. As such, each person is an atom, or cell, of the Divine. No other being has the privilege of free will, and therefore evil is an option, as is good. In this way we can sink or rise in the general unfolding of the Divine plan. *Elohim Creating Adam*, by William Blake, 1795.

particular feature of the pattern which in turn fitted into the grand design of the curtain.

The centerpiece of the Pargod is said to be the residence of the Messiah. This is the person, in each generation, who holds the position of being the connection between all the worlds, while living in the flesh. Who they are is only known to a small number of people on Earth, the *Lamed Vav*, the righteous "Thirty-Six," although he or she is known to the Great Holy Council of Heaven presided over by Metatron. This company of illuminated human beings is the spearhead of humanity, with the Messiah as its point of incarnate development.

One day the great eighteenth-century saint, the Baal Shem Tov, founder of the Hasidic movement in eastern Europe, was out driving a cart with a student. Suddenly they came to a halt by a cottage where the "Master of the Good Name" bowed to an old Jewish gentleman. Curious to know why his teacher should be so respectful, the student asked, as they drove away, who the man might be. The reply was "the Messiah."

HIDDEN WISDOM

ALL SOULS AND SPIRITS PRIOR
TO ENTERING THIS WORLD ARE
MADE UP OF MALE AND
FEMALE COMPONENTS
CONSTITUTING ONE BEING.
UPON DESCENDING TO THE
EARTH THEY SEPARATE AND
ANIMATE DIFFERENT BODIES.

Zohar

Previous page: All beings celebrate
Creation in a vision of Hildegard of
Bingen. The higher and invisible
worlds are accessible to humanity. We
are the only beings capable of entering
and existing simultaneously in all of
the four realities. It is quite possible
for an individual in a mystical state to
see the hosts of Heaven.

Everyone is born with a body. This contains the states of solids, liquids, gases and radiation as well as trace metals and minerals. It also has a vegetable component that can eat, drink, grow, propagate, age and die. The physical combination is completed by the animal soul, which has an instinctive intelligence and the ability to move about, socialize, express moods or exchange information. This set of vital capacities is called the *Nefesh* in Kabbalah. It is the driving force of most people's lives as they seek to live comfortably and have a pleasant social existence. However, there are those who wish to cultivate their humanity and find their place and purpose in the universe. After a long search such individuals eventually find a spiritual tradition which will instruct the seeker on the workings of the soul, the dynamics of the universe and their relationship to the Absolute.

The first lesson is that a human being is a miniature version of all Existence. An individual's body, psyche, spirit and Divine spark correspond to the macrocosm of the four worlds. Moreover, these innate levels are vehicles by which the aspirant can actually enter and experience the realms of *Asiyyah, Yezirah, Beriah* and *Azilut,* and so see the wider drama that they are a part of. Running in parallel to theoretical studies are the practices that will give them the discipline to cope with the powerful impact of direct cognition and illumination. These methods may be divided into the ways of Action, Devotion and Contemplation.

The first may be physical exercises and rituals, the second prayer

Scholars and their teacher, an
illustration from Maimonides' *Leader
of the Undecided Ones*, 1348. A
teacher is vital in Kabbalah to
instruct in the theory and practice of
the tradition. A school of the soul is
a group of people devoted to self and
mutual development as they become
companions of the spirit.

Illustrated Pentateuch
page with microscript
designs from the Yemen,
1469.

or meditations of the heart, while the third could be the intellectual study of metaphysics such as understanding the Divine Sefirot.

The degree of performance in all these ways will determine the development of the student. Over time the aspirant will be able to distinguish between the drives of the body, the impulses of the lower ego-Yesodic centered psyche and the higher state of consciousness of the inner Self, or the *Tiferet* pivot of the psychological Tree. Later, an awareness of the soul will emerge with insights into fate as the result of choice and temperament. After this comes the evolution of the transpersonal dimension of the spirit, which will reveal the student's destiny or work in the Divine scheme. During all these phases of development there may be moments of revelation and experience of the higher realms. There could be, in exceptional cases, a visitation by Elijah for advanced instruction. This is not so uncommon, as many distinguished Kabbalists down the centuries have reported or hinted at such a visitor.

Many Kabbalists speak of having a *Maggid*, or invisible teacher. This is sometimes called a guardian angel who protects as well as instructs. An angel, as said, is a messenger. These particular beings, however, are disembodied humans who act as tutors to the mystic. Some are long dead saints or sages, others of lesser caliber, depending upon the stage of the Kabbalist. Such entities often intervene in the lives of good people and especially children if they are in danger. They may or may not be seen, but their unearthly

Opposite: The inner life, like the outer one, is a constant struggle. Jacob, the ego, wrestles with the Self, symbolized by the Angel. After a long, dark night of the soul, he is renamed Israel—or "He who struggles with or for God." *Jacob's Fight with the Angel*, woodcut after a drawing by Gustave Doré.

presence is usually felt during or after a miraculous intervention.

The cumulative effect of generations of mystics of every tradition is slowly to increase humanity's awareness of the universe and God. Each esoteric line has its own methods, codes and metaphysics to bring about first individual illumination and then a mass evolution of souls. When this occurs, the Messiah will appear to all and the Days of Resurrection will begin. This means the rising up of the quick and dead, or the spiritually awake and asleep, for the final phase of Existence as mankind becomes conscious of all the worlds.

At this point people will be judged according to their overall performance as they turn towards their origin. As each individual ascends and fuses with his or her group into their place in Adam Kadmon, so this Divine image will increasingly realize whose likeness it reflects. When all the human sparks have united with the Ultimate Self, "I am that I am" will become One, as Face merges with Face. In that moment of completion, Existence will be but a glint in the eye of the Ancient of Ancients. The Holy One will be alone again, before perhaps beginning a new *Shmittah* or Great Cosmic Cycle.

BIBLIOGRAPHY

Bension, Ariel. *The Zohar in Spain.* New York: Herman Press, 1974.

Blumenthal, David. *Understanding Jewish Mysticism.* New York: Ktav, 1978.

Boker, Benzion. *The Jewish Mystical Tradition.* New York: Pilgrim Press, 1981.

Charles, R.H. *Book of Enoch.* London: SPCK, 1982.

Cordovero, Moses. *The Palm Tree of Deborah.* New York: Judaica Press, 1981.

Dan, Joseph. *Early Kabbalah.* New York: Paulist Press, 1986.

Epstein, Perle. *Kabbalah.* New York: Doubleday, 1978.

Frank, Adolphe. *The Kabbalah.* New York: University Books, 1967.

Ginsberg, Louis. *On Jewish Law and Lore.* New York: Atheneum, 1977. *Legends of the Bible.* Philadelphia: Jewish Publication Society, 1977.

Halevi, Z'ev ben Shimon. *Tree of Life. Way of Kabbalah. Psychology and Kabbalah.* New York: Weiser, all 1991. *A Kabbalistic Universe.* New York: Weiser, 1992. *Kabbalah: Tradition of Hidden Knowledge.* London: Thames and Hudson, 1992.

Jacobs, Louis. *Jewish Mystical Testimonies.* New York: Schocken, 1977.

Kaplan, Aryeh. *Bahir.* New York: Weiser, 1979. *Meditation and Kabbalah.* New York: Weiser, 1982. *Sefer Yezirah.* New York: Weiser, 1990.

Matt, Daniel C. *The Essential Kabbalah.* San Fransico: Harper SanFrancisco, 1995. Melzer, David. *The Secret Garden.* New York: Seabury Press, 1976.

Odeberg, Hugo. *Hebrew Book of Enoch*. New York: Ktav, 1973.

Schaya, Leo. *The Universal Meaning of Kabbalah*. London: Allen and Unwin, 1971.

Scholem, Gershom. *Kabbalah*. New York: Dorset Press, 1987 *Origins of Kabbalah*. Princeton: Jewish Publication Society, 1987. *Major Trends in Jewish Mysticism*. New York: Schocken Books, 1954.

Steinsaltz, Adin. *Thirteen Petalled Rose*. New York: Basic Books, 1981.

Tishby, Isaiah. *Wisdom of the Zohar*. Oxford: Oxford University Press, 1991.

Weiner, Herbert. *9 1/2 Mystics*. New York: Holt, Rinehart and Winston, 1969.

ACKNOWLEDGMENTS

AKG London: 3, 5, 7, 9, 10, 13, 15, 16, 17, 18, 23, 24, 33, 35, 37, 40, 43, 51, 55, 56, 59.
Abbey of St.Hildegard: 21, 39, 47, 53.
Warren Kenton: 1, 25, 27.
James Russell: frontispiece.
Sarajevo Haggadah: 30, 31, 34.
Tate Gallery, London: 48.
Juliette Soester: 38, 45.